PARIS, STAGE LEFT

KATE
NOAKES

PARIS, STAGE LEFT

EYEWEAR PUBLISHING

First published in 2017
by Eyewear Publishing Ltd
Suite 333, 19-21 Crawford Street
Marylebone, London W1H 1PJ
United Kingdom

Cover design and typeset by Edwin Smet
Author photograph by Marie de Lutz
Printed in England by TJ International Ltd, Padstow, Cornwall

ISBN 978-1-911335-42-9

*Eyewear wishes to thank Jonathan Wonham for his
generous patronage of our press.*

WWW.EYEWEARPUBLISHING.COM

a rose
is a rose
is a hip
as it goes

For Charlotte and Angharad

Kate Noakes lives and writes
in Paris and London. This is her
sixth collection. She is a Welsh
Academician and her website
boomslangpoetry.blogspot.com
is archived by the National
Library of Wales.

CONTENTS

I HISTORY

II TRAGEDY

III COMEDY

I
HISTORY

INTO L'ORANGERIE

I'm not ready to yield to the notion of garden
chalky-soft and muted, a green mat so bright
in the sun it silvers, jewels scribble flowers
life-size, bold, holding the year's nectar

but on dark days when river-wind over gravel
bites at my heels, chases me
I can see how it might work as I step unnoticed
over the brass rail and slip into the walls.

At pond's edge, my feet take root, my arms
branch and break into leaf, my fingertips
weep into the water. Purples and blues
are my last colours, air rushes my bark
and at sunset, I fire.

AFFECTING THE BALANCE

A loose cobblestone
fat as a lump of slow-
cooled basalt, a hazard
for stilt-walkers and girls
in the high-high heels
of now, or anyone disabled
unable, is the pavement
rebelling beneath our feet
rocking from sand
and mortar to flow as if
revivified, a lava stream
coursing the ancient ways
of the city, a rabble
discontented with its place.

Under traffic's drone
you can hear its troubles
the crack and spit
as hot stones hit the river.

RAPPING WHEN YOU DON'T KNOW THE WORDS OR THE STUPID THINGS AMERICAN TEENAGE BOYS SAY IN THE PLACE DES VOSGES

A found poem

I'm like, yeah, like, I actually, like, know a lot, like, about art.

She sees the same things as me.

I've got a tan line coming on.

If you fall asleep, it's gonna suck.

Why are all the houses here the same?

Let's fuck out.

She says, no when she means, yes.

PÊCHEURS

On damp days along Thames
and Loddon
where their wives can't see them
camouflaged men slouch
under out-sized umbrellas
waiting
for fish.

It's not easy telling the plash of rain
from signs of their prey.

Here, their hungry cousins sit
on crates
along the canal, hunched
against the wet
bearded
to hide their faces
real gnomes
wishing a kind well.

CROSSING PONT DE SULLY

to Quai de Tournelle to watch
the violin maker is to peer into amber

if he wasn't so obviously present
at his bench in the back of the shop.

He's up early to fine-grain spruce
or polish maple patiently

one layer of gloss
on another till it flames.

This is his business and ours
is not to fog the glass with our noses

though he's oblivious to the touch of ice.

HUQIN FOR ANNIE

A Chinese spike-fiddle
or whatever it's called, in my last
metro tunnel yesterday sounded
like a flute at first hearing; different

from the song the ancient Romany couple
play at the Pompidou, sometimes him
sometimes her taking turns to bow
or hold their lap dog by its rough coat

and I thought of your shiny Yamaha
you assure me is out of its case often
though I'm not there to hear it
but wish I was, so very much.

IT'S FIERCE, THE THING I HOLD

Thursday evenings I take my time
with a yellow cloth, dust off the curved
mahogany body, sinuous under my hand

your slim, tanned hips, firm-fleshed.
I hold its flame in the setting sun
think Crete, let it flare a little.

It bridges all emotion, ultra-violet
to infra-red, but only the willing can
hear this. I let it rest, tighten its strings

tuck it under my chin and pluck
and pluck till it plays true and clear
your honeyed voice.

All along my bow waits for love
the sweep of resin melting on its spine
rub of amber, enough to un-trap

the bees that buzz the metro stations
on Fridays, at dawn and dusk, charming
commuters to Mordor and back

into the sticky heart of the mountain
past the gold, and out, beyond.

WAKING TO BREAD

In the bake-house, gumminess fills
my nose with the warmth of yeast.
I can feel it rising in my mouth
the salt-melt-sweet.

> I eat my mother's breakfast: pastries.
> Too late for my *pain au chocolat* fix
> madame gives me *tarte aux poires* to taste
> with my *crème* – just a little bite, she winks.

Just one, Dad, my mum says, snagging
a fresh-piped cream horn from the tray.
It flakes her navy slip, coat, and seat
on the school train through the valley.

> Sugar round my mouth. We both lick our lips.

FRESH BREATH AND CONFIDENCE

The green drink, apothecary fluid
lurid in jars Taggatt's pharmacy window
after-school on my way to buy sweets
is probably *sirop de menthe*

no real plant gives liquor
of such hue to dye tongue, gullet, guts

or it acts in place of barium
highlighting blockages, shading other
indigestions I'd rather not consider.

I intrude into the mouths of
three women waiting for the train.
Their teeth are radioactive
and that's never a good thing.

WHEN THE TROUBADOUR

for Seamus Heaney

Not midwinter, nor midnight, not night, but
midsummer, no night and no night song

yet the blackbird is calling you, who take it
for lyricist, poet, part in competition

part accompaniment to a gathering
of far-from-home friends.

You mistake its knell, it is harbinger
of urgent words, irresistible –

gold the ferry-price, gold its beak
gold its molten throat, so you admit it

choose unplanned verses in praise
while its arrows dart your flesh

go tell, go tell.

YOU DON'T NEED LABELS

Where I live, the builders shout
at each other in a mixture of Arabic
and French. What shall I call this?
Frarabic? Ararench? It doesn't matter.

What matters is that if I'm there
to hear their voices bounce off
courtyard stone, I'm late, shouldn't be
at home, or am ill and should be.

My health is tempered by language
and the lullaby from a piano
played somewhere
in my building at all hours.

TRIG, PLACE DAUPHINE

The spring earth is dried
to red sand, hard enough
for the thud and clink of *pétanque*.

Metal chinks the lunchtime air
all ages of men adore the ground

measuring angles without rulers
hands on hips, triangulating.

I was always good at Trig and
it's the same, isn't it?

Distance, points, shortest.
What counts is the question of
weight and muscle between friends.

HORSES AND CLOTHES, VINCENT

are the only things that have changed in a century
the street is the same: benches, grills for tree roots
ironwork to protect their trunks, cafe tables, chairs
gossip and drink, box hedges have that pleasing
hip curve, carafes of water stand, coffee is drunk
conversation made, dogs are walked in parks
ground chalk, pea shingle, children play, are loved
old men carry sticks, old women cross cobbles
shops unfurl awnings, restaurants are posh
tablecloths are tablecloths, cutlery itself
there are umbrellas, it rains, the sky is blue
night black, light glows yellow, shadows fall
skirts are shorter, no stiff folds of cloth, no fur trims
except on the woman in full-length black mink
this morning and me, out of green paint, only able
to make a hiss with my teeth she didn't understand
looked at me as if I needed carting to an asylum.

SUR L'HERBE

It's bad enough being stripped naked before lunch
so these hungry men can argue the toss
about the fall of light on my breasts
whether it's clearer on the left or right
but they've been long enough for the brie to run
and the bread to dry to a crisp.

All I want is to eat
and fix the black silk ribbon in my hair.
They're obsessed, but you, Edouard, find time
to fly a bullfinch through the summer wood
just we two catch the flash, its rosy chest.

MELUSINE AT CHÂTELET

A mirror-tiled morning, she's bare-tailed
in a metro tunnel, toes fused and splayed

each foot a flipper displayed
to half a million passers-by, who fail

to see her in her damp, hair-tangled days,
but know they're off course from siren song.

Who will come now to carry her along
to dive into the light of this wide bay?

BUNTINGS

Small birds, legs-a-blur, skittering
from us along the shingle
their scrape nests
safe from our tramp feet
palm sized, perfect
disguised in their beach coats
breasts white as spume.

Funny to think of them as my train
speeds the snow fields in the dark.
Connections.
Best not to fathom.

TRUFFLES

Sunday
a new stallholder calls me
to trays of dark earth and plenty
saffron trumpets, fat boletus, fleshy
under brown caps
and handfuls of truffles.

Before I part with cash
I need to nose a few things, so please
be kind enough to let me judge
the tension in your eyes
and at the corners of your mouth.

The source is crucial, as it's so early
in the season and these black tubers
packed in plastic barquettes
weighed, labeled,
have yet to reach their fullest perfume.

The breed of the dank-smelling sow is
important, but mostly I want to be sure
that, unlike much else
these diamonds of the kitchen
were not made pungent in China.

MIST, FRUIT, BLOOD

Autumn proper, air softens, nip-nip,
greys All Soul's dome with its tears.

Smooth for now, apples shine.
Come buy. Come buy. We must/must not.

They're ready for incision, flesh-bite,
a crunch like fracturing bone

and the flick of my tongue tip against
poison pills, pip-pip. Ah, yes. Hallowe'en.

Ah yes, Hallowe'en. Harvest moon lands
on a stall in a thud-thump of pumpkins,

their skin no guide to their shade,
slice-slice, nor their size or shape,

you can't predict the dark side.
A Turks? I hoist a tri-colour, but sage

beyond her years, she shakes her head
Jack-o-lanterns don't come from Istanbul.

We take the smoothest and, knife-knife,
I stay late to carve it Kruger.

SHRAPNEL

Autumn, his plough folds the land
flattens mounds, fills trenches, yet
the lines are indelible.
In winter, thin ponds form
in summer, the clay shrinks
from boards and props.

Some years he doubles back
to level the fields, new steel
just turns up the old, not gull food
inedible scraps, no magpie
glitter in bullet cases
snips of barbed wire, bits of shells.

History's not erased by work
still he tries to ditch the ghosts.
It's hard not to see them
from the corner of his eyes.
There, the white plot fenced by firs
daily sight of that great loss.

SAVE THE FEATHER FOR YOUR HAT

Waterloo, of course
another battle, a concourse
the crowd, heading here, heading home
a young woman, of course, another battle
easy to spot on the concourse
there in her mother's plumed hat.

Too many little egrets died
for her mother's plumed hat
another battle, there on the concourse
too many to tremble the felt
with each rise of her head
a young woman, easy to spot, of course
home there in the crowd at Waterloo.

Of course, she hunts the concourse
without sense, her simple face rising
easily for another battle, framed here
by the white aigrettes of her mother's
plumed hat, a young woman there
head spotting the Waterloo crowd.

Easy, another battle, mad to me now
of course, as mad as Waterloo, Alice, honey
as church bells and afternoon tea
a woman, young, on the concourse
spotted there in her mother's plumed hat
with a crowd of dead egrets
here simple and senseless.

She singles me in the crowd
the young woman on the concourse
another battle headed here
in her mother's plumed hat, though
one easy look at my trembling hands
of course, would've told her: head home
spot there another Waterloo man.

RUE PAVÉE

Every day I pass within two inches of a gun.

Some mornings I turn to avoid it.
Don't spook the soldier, who's slung it
across his chest. Finger on trigger. Ready.

Sometimes he says *Bonjour.* I smile.
He nods his bereted head.
He's young. Enough to be my son.

Some days he's a young woman.
There for my safety on the narrows
between synagogue and school.

Reminder, war isn't somewhere else.

SHOULDER TO SHOULDER

I do not ask why.
I deny you understanding
credence, acceptance.

Because, because, because.

I already know
you make no sense.

★

Je ne demande pas pourquoi.
Je vous nie compréhension
crédibilité, acceptance.

Pourquoi, pourquoi, pourquoi.

Je sais déjà
vous êtes sans sens, sans sensibilité.

II
TRAGEDY

PONT DE SÈVRES

The night river, all gilt muscle
under a ripped velvet glove
you say is beautiful
in a vague hand-waving way.

I say I'm cold. What I mean is
I'm as freezing as thin porcelain.
Your cruelty
chips and cuts me.

It's painful asking you
for a favour.
I wish you'd take a dive
from the bridge, let the water
swallow you.

I could add tin to your pockets
galena ore, give you a push,
watch you glaze
and try to swim. But

I need walking to the Metro.
It's late. Get me safely in.

NOT FOREVER, ONLY NOW

Because
three men with varying states of alopecia
the pharmacy signs are disco green, flashing
home from gymnastics, a girl is spinning a white hoola hoop
a graffitied van is hauled on a break-down lorry, hydraulics hissing metal
a baby in a backpack is bored, toasty and teething
a post-party boy is engrossed by balloon animals
of admonishments for those speaking *anglais*
bling on a pierced top lip, a stapled eyebrow
a second hand fur coat and enough tobacco to give everyone cancer
there is always the eye and the men giving it
working girls clank keys
men wearing women's scarves are making mistakes
the happy man dances without headphones
there have to be two chairs at each table so no-one ever is alone
people talking have much to say
there is grit on my face, and
you did not say goodbye.

THE MATTRESS

we found   thrown out   on street
its difficult   shape weight
we not move   every day
only when police say

it was clean   park dust
chalk   concrete   cover us
grubby I try   I try
make home   under sky

Lucca works   casual
cash   wash up   usual
food   food   is all we think
days nothing   hot drink

we fit it all   sleep here
little ones   so small   hear
how long   how long for
hard making home   in door

some people kind   kind   kind
wake up morning   coins find
baker   left over bread
full dream   fills belly   head

angry shopkeepers   mean
shout at us   throw things   scream
kids scared   don't know   ask why
making home   under sky.

STAY HERE LONG ENOUGH AND YOU WILL START TO FEEL COLD

If there is light in knowing, mole-girl chose
not to see it, lived her own darkness
seldom reminded herself of the scent
of damp leaves, the slide of tamped clay
under her feet, soft soil taste of earth food.

Life sounds rarely echoed from above
tractor gears grinding, the screech of gull
and crow, low moans of byre-bound cattle.
She recalled less clearly each day the tap
of crop roots extending, had only car horns
the shouts of corn men, to show she wasn't alone.

She met no-one in the humming corridors
of the Metro, let its night fall filthy
around her. Life was not at the end
of a field drain, no tiled tunnel led home.
She woke on a fence post choking
her hedge noose tightened.

COQ AU VIN, OR
THE WAY WITH A MAN

Rooster, not young, not old
full scarlet combed and proud

and first taking care
to catch and keep every tear

(you will need those after
to remember you lover)

pair chopped with sweet shallots,
bitter herbs, rich claret,

quick sear, seal, sauce, then stew,
this dear one is what to do.

I'M SENT FOR MEAT, A REAL MAN'S JOB

I slip on iced puddles
that pond the gutters
and the small deer slides
from my back
the hares from my grip

but I'm a heavy lifter.
Jug. Jug.
The gall will thicken
and she'll bring plenty
with a mad smile.

All we've had is rabbit meat.

We chance to die
today, tomorrow.
If my eyes are blue
my ears boxed black
there's no surprise.

That's lucky
her tongue a fist
her fist, itself.
Jug. Jug.
Bring me the bloody hind.

IN MY COLD BLOOD, CALCULATING

I've always thought revenge
a dish of strawberry blancmange
in school the kind we joked was left
over from the war that we ate
by the tray load, *every last spoonful*
our bowls empty, scraped clean
mouths clagging, nothing
left for the pig swill, and that had
a tinge of powder to it
never smooth on the tongue
and easy to swallow as something
one might eat after a tonsillectomy
it had a thick skin and bitter
after taste, as if the odd leaf or pip
had been bound in the mix
and was perhaps a kind poison.
Crème caramel anyone?

THE DESTRUCTION OF ANNOYING ANIMALS

And here, we are not just talking nuisance
as in occasional pest that bites once, irritates
for a short while and then disappears
such as a party-snore or holiday snapper
no, I mean someone more insidious
and skin-burrowing, who despite your
best attempts at avoidance, leaving early
arriving late, is somehow always there
wherever you go and turns up like a bad penny
bent for fun at *Ripley's Believe It Or Not*
and have kept in your purse for years
a totem that doesn't seem to have brought you
any luck and certainly not the ability to rid
yourself of this annoying animal
such that there is only one solution
and that involves a well-timed trip to
Julien Aurouze and his marvelous emporium
of poisons and traps at 8 rue des Halles
open Monday to Saturday, nine to six thirty
closed for lunch from twelve thirty to two
where you will find the cure for your problem
whether that is an itch of fleas, a trip of mice
an hotel of cockroaches, a kit of pigeons
or this particularly troublesome and singular
nest of rats whose heads you can gleefully imagine
desiccated and strung in the shop window
as warning for the next hundred years.

SCOLD

All this blah blah is filming my tongue

as if I've drunk a litre of full-fat
and it's globules have blocked the pores

slowed the muscle to a milk slug

sliming between my teeth
crying enough, enough.

All this blah blah is stopping my tongue

as if I've swallowed plaster of Paris
and its setting heat has fixed the muscle

firmed it for a few weeks, making me rest

then, freed it when silence
has been enough, enough.

All this blah blah has bled my tongue

as if every word is a drop
congealing on the rough post

where it's been nailed, because I refused

my son, told the recruiters
enough, enough.

ALL SOULS' DAY

Quick and true, an arrow from beak to tail
this fine heart of feathers scans clouded sky
and the Mansard roofs from my high chimney.

Ready with its supply of plump pigeons
the city is packed with Peregrine game
and he likes their breast meat well enough
to stay long by my window.

Viciousness comes in so many colours
even white, with spots or stripes, this man
has talons, is expert, knows how to draw
and syphon blood, rip flesh, leave me, out, dry.

STROLL, PELOUSE INTERDIT

Poems from the Marais gardens, 2014

I INSTITUTE SUÈDOIS

The one-eyed crow is sharp
makes his point with gore, not
his bill, caws a little acid at me.

Even the spear-headed hydrangeas
agree with necessary statements
point to innocence lost

and the difficulty of deckchairs.

The yew reddens into secrets
shadows creep across the grass
ants feast on my legs.

II HOTEL LAMOIGNON

Stop Go
Stop Go Go

Stop Stop Go

Go Stop
Go Go Stop

Go Stop Stop

these lights hesitate

Go Stop Go
installation of stalling

yet there is/was no orange
no warning, no preparation
just the Stop Go Stop

no pause, wait, think

Look Left
Look Right
Looking and Listening
as you cross

no chance to try again.

III SQUARE BARYE

Nothing comes from dust, dust
more dust, sea creatures crushed
chalk my soles in their millions.

The statue is all muscle lion, male
can be turned to dust in a few swift blows
loaded, barged, dumped somewhere down river.

The water faces the wrong way, evening light
caught on the wake, the pilot blind
everyone somewhere else

except a resting runner and me, kicking
my heels, wiping grit from my eyes.

No stone is more than another, no flesh
higher, all is dust, returns to dust
and this place is no place to decide anything.

IV ANNE FRANK

It would be mean
to say cliché
next to the museum
of art and history
but I can't help it
must be the doll's eyes

and yes, the world is stone
stone, stoned, the murdered
and me still dead

no matter how many
rowans you plant
or how jolly the bunting.

V ARCHIVES

Blousy as garnet hydrangeas
in formality run casual

Pisceans like myself
are in the wild parterre

box melanged with geraniums
sedums, corn cockles

in the balance we try to hold
between our two sides

the serious, the crazy

where only some pigeons
take off, about half the time.

VI JARDIN DES ROSSIERS

This mad grass, miscanthus
is taller and greyer than me.

There's an Alice thing here
makes me long for cake, gallons

of tea and a river bank snooze
but a rustle of silver birch, the grunts

of a child uprooting a wooden
mushroom, its caterpillar long gone

vanish the Thames
and I'm trapped in this maze

of narrow streets where there's
never enough water running.

VII PLACE DES VOSGES

In all seasons I have sat
under this pleached bower
year on year, waiting
for a love that never came.

Lime has made a bitter cordial
sugar spoonfuls no medicine.
I've been a fool.

The bins fill with water
when it rains. The winter
lawn needs its little rest.

Cleaned fountains and spring
are always a lifetime away.

VIII MUSÉE CARNAVALET

Pause. Let traffic cede, move
to soft beds changed with the season
remember ancestors, gunpowder
glowing in these bright mounds.

Autumn is rust, purple, crimson, gold
imperial blooms in the gloam
and noisy flow of a year
you can almost hear turning.

A motorbike. Paper torn
from the book, ripped in two
and again and again and again

shredded, its story remnant
only in scraps, these tear-shapes
petals jewelling twilight stones today
tomorrow their shine faded.

IX JARDIN PARTAGE DU CLOS DES BLANCS MANTEAUX

Browned, brittled, Horse Chestnuts
have given up against leaf miners
for another year, have let
this invasion conquer them.

It's hard not to crumple
under the beat of pigeons' wings
knowing there's one long-fingered
half-red chili and if you touch it
and wipe your eyes you'll be
in terrible trouble.

Better settle for what you are
a freshly clipped lavender.

X SQUARE GEORGE CAIN

My bronzed chest
breasts the potager

I look out in a beam
that's not trained on me

and the trailing nasturtiums
but focused on brilliance

those spots when I flash
yellow to red

like their peppery flowers
warning   warning

this is not over, it's not time
to harvest the ruby chard.

XI SQUARE LEOPOLD-ACHILLE

Ox-blood stucco falls away
in chunks from particular walls

mistaken for Virginia creeper in her last coat
it's swept up, bagged, taken away

to wherever away is
the place for stacking the past
sealing it away

but not so tight as to preserve it.
In time it will fall away.

They tell me a cigarette butt takes
fifty years to fade away
in my case thirty-two.

I've been early to the party, always.

BEFORE I CAN WALK AGAIN

I do not remember how many
pairs of boots are in the wardrobe
or how many need re-heeling
or the number of summer dresses I own
that actually fit, or before you no longer
wanted to, the number of nights
you slept in my bed.

I don't recall the number of hours
I can stare out of the window
at pigeons and crows, or the weeks
the Pantheon's been scaffolded
and sheeted, or how many nights
I've listened to music to herald sleep
or how many I've not.

I don't remember the number
of socks and earrings
I've lost, or necklaces I've broken
or how long the nights
I've slept alone
or, how long those nights
I will sleep, alone.

I AM WEARING LAYERS AND DO NOT SHIVER

Thin light. You expect me to kneel down
and put my head on the block.

*Legend: Anne Boleyn was given the mercy
of a sharp sword, and skill, a swift blow.*

A trial where the witch is not allowed to speak.
Something mediaeval in your methods.

The outcome foregone. A show for your conscience
where history's rewritten in a hurry. A conclusion.

*Legend: It took two goes to sever Mary, Queen
of Scot's head from her neck. Chop. Chop.*

A trump of lies. A packed-up charge sheet.
The impossibility of proving the positive.

The possibility of disproving the negative.
Science has it so.

*Legend: Marie-Antoinette apologised
for treading on her executioner's toe.*

You were given plenty of rope, but because
you didn't treat me like a queen, you missed.

The failed hangman keeps the boots.
Be ready with the polish.

JE SUIS UNE AUTRE

My dear friend says
with the gift of language
I should sing the good world
our bad-bad times
but I'm not a town crier.

My mouth's full of cotton rags.
I'm tone deaf.
So, forgive me
if all I can do today
is hum a little, honey.

SIGNS AND OTHER CONCERNS

When the national icon is lit
in the colours of the flag
it signals what, exactly?

When one third of the flag is blue
you can feel cold and calculation
shiver your bones.

When another is red, you can reckon
on blood such there's not enough
sawdust for the pavements.

When only a third of the flag is white
peace is never assured.

III
COMEDY

FIND ME A COMPLIANT TIGER SO I CAN TAKE MY PICK

A domed temple on the Ile de la Jatte,
an upstream romance:
fluted pillars of warm stone,
yellowed with lichen, pocked with soot,
a good place to find home.

I know its Georgian twin after
the bridge at Henley as well as
my love's arm on my bones
same rounded, sandy oolite
carvings, smuts of coal.

Choose your river and choose wisely –
eeny meany, eeny meany,
eeny meany, miney mo.

K IS WORTH FIVE POINTS

The first three words you spot
in the puzzle tell you most.

On Concorde's tiles where giant letters
stride the walls in ten-league boots

I face these choices: liberty
liberty, liberty.

One luxury on the desert island
so I take dominion over

myself, me, myself, I.

THE CITY, MY HEADLESS LOVER

Mighty at the north his chest lies
between Chaumont and Montmartre
which holds his heart and mine.
I can rest there in the dark.

In the eastern and western woods
his feet stretch and put down roots.
It's just a question of choosing
a side to start.

The wide boulevards make a house
for his strong limbs. The river
snakes silver between them
and I glide and I glide.

ANOTHER REASON WHY I DON'T NEED
A GLOW IN THE DARK BUBBLE MAKER

The flowers are lovely
really they are
but you've made a mistake

the man I'm talking to
outside this bar
is not the kind
to buy me roses
of any sort, so far.

PULLING THE LAPTOP FROM THE FRONT COMPARTMENT OF MY SUITCASE

I take with it a pair of yesterday's knickers
black ones.
They could be a cleaning cloth for sunglasses
large ones.
I stuff them back.

There are men interested in such.
I look around
but don't see any.
I'm in Paris, and they are mainly
in Japan on street corners
selecting schoolgirls' panties
pre-worn, from vending machines.

I recall a friend in Tokyo
once in need of fresh underwear.

LET ME GIVE YOU A TIP

One might ask why, but
if you're going to have sex
on a hot day, as well as the curtains
do close the windows.

My elderly neighour likes
to go to bed before ten
and her way of making you stop
is to ask, *are you all right?*

Not unreasonable, as you
sound in terrible pain, or as if
you're beating a Jack Russell
with a short, sharp, stick.

THE FATTEST WOOD PIGEONS IN PARIS LIVE IN THE GERANIUM PLANTER ON MY BALCONY

beak twig he
nest weave she

coo coo he
sit sit she

look quietly
move slowly

eye beady
me watching

her watching
me

LOST, IF SPOTTED, PLEASE CALL

Somewhere in the Marais
you lost your cockatiel.

How does this happen, losing a pet?

A dog, yes, might slip its lead
after an attractive scent

a cat, being of its own mind
and unfathomable, does as it pleases.

It's not that you lose it, more
it loses you, chooses.

But a bird, loosing its cage door
when the window is open.

Are you sure you didn't mean it?

FATBITCHFROMHELL

stood on my toes today, *putain*,
both her clumpy boots planted
on my ballerinas. It hurt. A lot.

Especially my right big toe
with its crushed bones
from the too-close encounter

with the base of the espresso machine.
I swore at her roundly
and in English. She got the point.

Pardon and *désolée* not enough
not nearly. Fatbitchfromhell – diet
and hold on to something, next time.

I FOUND AN EGG ON THE METRO

Well, not so much found
this was no Easter Sunday hunt
for secreted, foiled and chocolate ova
more found as in almost trod in.

Makes a change, I thought,
from all the dog shit, piss
and round plates of fresh vomit.
Odd. Why would anyone crack an egg?

It's not warm enough down there to fry.
No sign of the shell though.

THINGS YOU NEVER HEAR FRENCH PEOPLE SAY (NO. 65)

I'm sorry

I'm sorry I'm on a train and

I'm sorry I'm on a train and if I cut

out please forgive me

forgive me

BON WEEKEND

It's rough, a working man/woman's bar. The kind of place if at home I'd not be seen dead in as I am *un peu snob*. Because I am not at home it has the taint of the exotic, from the Moroccan barmen to the aged wood. Everything is other and old. There are two stickers from Chirac's last run and the poster for a new album from 2008. But the price of tagines and cocktails has increased, and the smoke is vapour. It's Friday. I'm waiting for you to step off the train. There are few options in this part of town. I've got the beginnings of a cold and I've just soaked my peanuts with whisky. I don't think I asked for a double, but I got one anyway. *Ça, n'est pas grave.* A nice Frenchman is coming to meet me to pass the hour. I sip and fire rekindles my belly. He's late, of course.

COUNTING WITH BAGUETTES

One

Quotidian lover or baby, tucked against breast
it rises with Laurence's breath, batons her heart.

Two

As ears, fingers grow with age. No practice
needed to manage twin sticks singlehanded
says Claire, brandishing the second batch.

Three

Right hand, a triplet of orange carrier bags,
left can't cope with a triumvirate of loaves.
There must be a body trick between chest and fist
but not one Stephane has learned. His tradition
speaks no evil: the number of times they fall.

IF ONLY I HAD MY BASEBALL BAT

Although not fitting for this fake Prada bag,
the rat was the size of a Chihuahua.

Bold as a monkey it paused, mid-arch
to outstare me, dare me,

but sick with fever I wasn't tricked
wouldn't play its black eyed, beady game

though my toes in their spiked boots
stretched, and started to itch.

THERE ARE FEW LARGE DOGS IN PARIS

Is it human? I ask side-
stepping a rivulet of late-night piss.

Yup, you point, obviously.

Two metres on *Bavaria* cans lie empty
on the opera steps.

So much for Rhinegold, I quip.
You hum Valkyrie through pursed lips.

IT GOES LIKE THIS

An elegant woman, slim, long
dark hair, tanned from an early holiday
comes to the gate of a posh block of flats.

An older woman, plump, walks
with a stick, returning from the boulangerie
arrives at the gate at the same time.

The younger holds the gate open
while the dog on her pink lead
gets in the way, somewhat.

Passing each other, the two women
exchange a few words for the morning.
The elder goes in.

As the younger starts her walk
the dogs pulls away to the nearest grass
not a lawn, a rebellious patchwork

coming up through hexagonal blocks
around a plane tree.
She leaves a small deposit.

The elegant woman ignores it
no spare hands, lead, fag
and anyway, it's just the start.

HONESTLY THIS YEAR

I am going to behave and stop staring
at strange men on the metro

the badly-dressed and poorly shod
the bloody-shaved, the hairy sods

the pierced with Staffies on strings
the skull-tattooed with lip rings

the ones with wired heads, especially them
appearing now more fools than men

the space-starers, the lap sitters
the nose pickers, the ball scratchers

the man-bag wearers
putain, the swearers.

Yes, I'm going to stop staring at men.

THANKS ALL THE SAME

I'll have the guide to cheap eats please.

I could have taken the history of famous
monuments, parks and gardens, but
it's winter and I'm planning
on hibernating with a full stomach.

SHOW ME THE GRID

said one metro trader to his rival on a dank evening at *République*. I need to know if artificial hibiscus those useful light up wands are urgent and important or just urgent and not important.	You're sure they're not just not urgent, but important?
Not, not either, I'd say. Only fluffy battery-powered puppies fall into that square. It's the way they yap on the old shoe box lid at intervals repelled by its rim.	Perfectly. That's the preserve of leather belts and CDs on the same tarpaulin for some reason, genius.

FABULOUS

They say at fifty women acquire
a super power, invisibility –
if true it would be handy discovering
what people really think, friends, for example.

I must be doing something wrong, as
the man who shucks oysters at the corner,
snuggles them into beds of ice, notices me
clearly; he looks up, smoulders *Bonjour*

as does the guy who envisages coffee
with me each day before work, as any chap
spying me alone on a bar stool
in my violet heels. And the boy from Bombay

sends me his deepest love thirty odd years
after I dumped him for this best friend.
You don't do that to thin air. What they say
is a lie, or my passport has a typo.

AFTER THIRTY YEARS, MORE

Wars have been over in
less time than
it's taken me
to pluck up the courage.
I can hardly believe
you are here
and yet
here you are
with those same green eyes
from a life ago
smiling
saying nothing's changed
save time on our faces.
It isn't a dream.
Pinch me.

Pinch me.
It isn't a dream
save time on our faces.
Saying nothing's changed
smiling
from a life ago
with those same green eyes
here you are
and yet
you are here.
I can hardly believe
to pluck up the courage
it's taken me
more time than
wars have been over in.

AUBADE

I picture waking to a man
the one in the next room, softly
playing the piano that isn't there.

He tenders its keys into song
fingers as gentle on the ivory
as my skin, their pressure fluent.

The melody caresses my limbs
into cat-stretch. I listen
before moving more.

Day's breaking dream fades.
The piece ends.
I wait.

THIS IS US THEN

with our grown up jobs,
grown up waistlines
and grown old
grown out hair

meeting in grown up places
like five-star hotel lobbies
one-star restaurants
and champagne bars where
no-one asks our age

writing grown up texts
with capitals, whole words
punctuation.

This is us snogging
at railway stations
like giddy teenagers
we did that before

demanding very politely
a change of room when
king-size has grown small

grown up enough to order
food after the kitchen
has closed, and care if the maid
curses our wrecked bed.

PLACE DE L'OPÉRA

The next day, by fortune, I stood
on the spot at Café de la Paix
where we kissed and parted

and waited for the muses
to shower me with gifts

as if the pavement held the print
of you and the air could be stilled
by your soul left behind

as if a discarded butt could be
your breath or a crumpled flyer
your last word, happy.

I stood there, to see
if I could conjure you again
in a gilded rain.

Was that your hand on my back?
Sun on my face, a kiss of sorts
the murmur of cars, a whisper.

Happy, yes I shall be
Danäe, and be happy.

IN THIS PLACE, KRISHNA

There should be a plaque
to us here
where you kissed me

and here
where we swallowed
oysters and you kissed me

and here
where we drank
cocktails and you kissed me

and here
where we walked, fingers
entwined and you kissed me

and here
where we marveled the moon
and you kissed me

and here
where we slept deep
dreaming and you kissed me

and here
and here
and here

where you kissed me
till my body
was tinged with blue.

YES

Nothing moves
not the ice floes
not the branches.

Shadows of beech trunks
barcode the canal.

The world holds
its breath, paused
on the cusp of change.

I wait. One whisper
of your lips on my neck.

Come closer love
the word you seek is
yes.

OTHER BOOKS BY KATE NOAKES

Tattoo on Crow Street, Parthian (2015)
I-spy and Shanty, Corrupt Press (2013)
Cape Town, Eyewear Publishing (2012)
The Wall Menders, Two Rivers Press (2009)
Ocean to Interior, Mighty Erudite (2007)

ACKNOWLEDGEMENTS

Earlier versions of these poems have appeared in *Belleville Park Pages* ('I found an egg on the metro'), *Ink Sweat & Tears* ('Into L'Orangerie' and 'I Am Wearing Layers And I Do Not Shiver'), *Magma* ('Scold'), *Poetry Ireland Review* ('Before I Can Walk Again'), *Poetry Wales* ('I'm sent for meat, a real man's job'), *Tears in the Fence* ('Mist, fruit, blood'), *The North* ('Pont de Sèvres'), *The Stare's Nest* ('Affecting The Balance').

'Save the feather for your hat' was anthologised by Two Rivers Press (*The Arts of Peace*) in 2014. 'Melusine at Chatelet' was anthologized in *Lines Underwater* in 2013. 'The mattress' was anthologized by the University of London (*Human Rights*) in 2013.

'Rapping when you don't know the words' was written for Michelle McGrane's online poetry project, *Against Rape*, at the Peony Moon website in 2014.

I thank their editors here.

EYEWEAR PUBLISHING